The Boy Who Cried Wolf

Retold by Jenny Giles
Illustrated by Naomi C. Lewis

Once upon a time,
a boy named Josef lived with his family
in a small village.

There were high hills all around
the village, and away in the distance
there was a dark forest.

Josef was learning to be a shepherd boy.
On his first morning,
he had to take the sheep
up to a high meadow all by himself.

2

3

As Josef sat and watched the sheep,
he looked across at the dark forest.
His father had said to him,
"If you see a wolf coming
out of the forest, you must call me.
I will bring the men from the village
to help you chase it away."

The day went by very slowly,
and Josef grew bored and lonely.
He grew tired of looking at the sheep
and watching out for the wolves.

At long last, the sun went down
and he could walk home with the sheep.

Early the next morning,
Josef had to take the sheep
up to the meadow again.
The day went by even more slowly.
Then, as he sat watching the sheep,
an idea came to him.

"If I pretend that a wolf
is coming out of the forest,
someone will come running
up here to see me," he said to himself.
So Josef shouted down to his father,
"Help me!   A wolf is coming
to get the sheep. **Wolf!   Wolf!**"

Josef's father quickly called
the village men together.
They picked up heavy sticks
and rushed up the hill
to help Josef.

But when they got to the meadow,
there was no wolf to be seen.
Josef said, "The wolf went away
when it heard you coming!"
The men were glad
that the wolf had disappeared.
They stayed and talked to Josef
for a while, and then they all went
back to work.

But the next day,
Josef played the same trick again.
"Come and help me!" he called.
"I can see a wolf. **Wolf! Wolf!**"

Again the men ran up the hillside
to the meadow.
"Where is the wolf?" they asked.
"We cannot see any wolves!"
And with that, they all went
back down to the village.

The following day,
Josef cried *Wolf* again.
But this time, when the men came
and found no wolf,
they were angry with Josef.

"You have called us
three times now," they said,
"and we have never seen a wolf.
We don't believe you anymore,
and we are not going to come
if you call *Wolf* again."

13

So the next morning,
when Josef walked up
to the meadow with the sheep,
he knew that he had
a long, lonely day ahead of him.

Then, as he looked over
at the forest,
he saw a dark shadow
moving out of the trees.
It was a wolf!
And more dark shadows
were following it!

Josef was very frightened.

He shouted down to the village.

"Wolf! Wolf! I can see a wolf!"

But the people just went on
with their work.

"We are not going to be tricked again,"
they said to each other.

Josef was terrified.

He ran down the hillside shouting,

"Help me! Help me!

The wolves are coming out of the forest.

They will get the sheep!"

But no one paid any attention to Josef.

He had tricked them too many times.

Josef's father said, "Come with me, Josef.

I will take you back up the hillside.

You must look after the sheep."

But when Josef and his father
reached the meadow,
they saw a terrible sight.
The wolves had killed most of the sheep.
"No one came to help me!" cried Josef.
"No one listened to me!"

His father turned to him and said,
"You cried *Wolf* too many times
when there was no wolf.
So when the wolves really came,
no one believed you!"

Josef felt very sad, and very, very sorry
about what he had done.

And from that moment on,
Josef knew he must
always tell the truth
so that people could believe him,
and trust him.

A play
The Boy Who Cried Wolf

People in the play

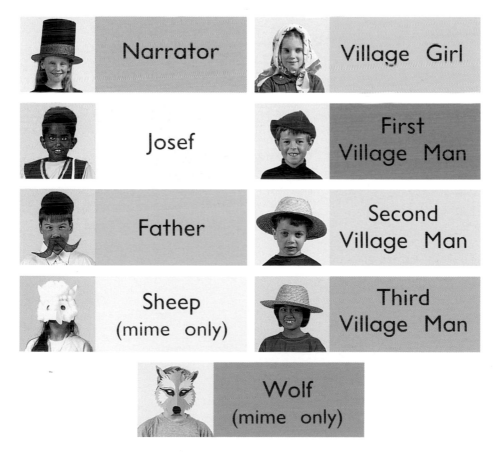

Narrator		Village Girl	
Josef		First Village Man	
Father		Second Village Man	
Sheep (mime only)		Third Village Man	
Wolf (mime only)			

Narrator

Once upon a time,
a boy named Josef lived with his family
in a small village.
There were high hills
all around the village,
and away in the distance
there was a dark forest.

Josef was learning to be
a shepherd boy.
On his first morning,
he had to take the sheep
up to a high meadow all by himself.

Father

You must sit and watch our sheep
all day, Josef.
Do not let them go out of the meadow.

Josef

I will look after the sheep, Father,
and when the sun goes down,
I will bring them home.

Father

There are wolves in the forest, Josef.
If you see a wolf coming out of the forest
to get the sheep, you must call me.
I will bring the men from the village
up to the meadow
to help you chase it away.

Narrator

Josef sat and watched the sheep.
The day went by very slowly.

Josef

Oh, I am so bored and lonely.
I am tired of watching the sheep,
and looking out for wolves.
I will be glad when the sun goes down
and I can walk home with the sheep.

Narrator

Early the next morning,
Josef had to take the sheep
up to the meadow again.
The day went by even more slowly.
Then, as Josef sat watching the sheep,
an idea came to him.

Josef

If I pretend that a wolf is coming
out of the forest, someone will come
running up here to see me.

Narrator

So Josef shouted down to his father.

Josef

Help me! A wolf is coming
to get the sheep. **Wolf! Wolf!**

Village Girl

Joseph has seen a wolf!

Father (to the village men)

Come with me! Josef has seen a wolf!
We must go up to the meadow
and help him!

First Village Man

We will come with you.

Second Village Man

We must take some heavy sticks with us.

Third Village Man
We will help chase the wolf away.

Narrator
But when they got to the meadow,
there was no wolf to be seen.

Josef
The wolf went away
when it heard you coming!

First Village Man
That's lucky!

Second Village Man
We must have frightened it away.

Third Village Man
We can go back to work now.

Father

You can bring the sheep home later,
Josef, when the sun goes down.

Narrator

But the next day,
Josef played the same trick again.
He called down to his father...

Josef

Come and help me!
I can see a wolf! **Wolf! Wolf!**

Father (to the village men)

Josef has seen the wolf again!
We must go and help him.

Narrator

Again the men ran up the hillside
to the meadow.

First Village Man

Where is the wolf?

Second Village Man

I cannot see any wolves!

Third Village Man

I am going back to work in the village.

Father

The wolf has gone away, Josef.
You will be safe now.

Narrator

And Josef's father went back
to the village with the men.

The following day, Joseph called
down to the village again.

28

Josef
Wolf! Wolf! The wolf is coming!

Narrator
But this time, when the men came and found no wolf, they were angry with Josef.

First Village Man
You have called us three times now and we have never seen a wolf.

Second Village Man
We don't believe you anymore!

Third Village Man
We are not coming to help you again.

Narrator
But the next day, when Josef looked over at the forest, he saw a dark shadow moving out of the trees.

Josef
A wolf is really coming out of the forest.
I must call down to the village!

Narrator
Josef was very frightened.

Josef
Wolf! Wolf! I can see a wolf.

First Village Man
We are not going to listen to Josef.

Second Village Man
We are not going to be tricked again.

Narrator
Josef was terrified.
He ran down the hillside.

Josef

Help me! Help me!

The wolves are coming out of the forest.

They will get the sheep!

Narrator

But no one paid any attention to Josef.

He had tricked them too many times.

Father

Come with me, Josef.

I will take you back up the hillside.

You must look after the sheep.

Narrator

But when Josef and his father reached
the meadow, they saw a terrible sight.
The wolves had killed
most of the sheep.

Josef

No one came to help me!
No one listened to me!

Father

You cried *Wolf* too many times
when there was no wolf, Josef.
So when the wolves really came,
no one believed you!

Josef

I am very sorry for what I have done,
Father.

Narrator

And from that moment on,
Josef knew he must always tell the truth
so that people could believe him,
and trust him.